G000066519

JACKIE

JACKIE

JULIE MARS

Ariel Books

Andrews and McMeel

Kansas City

Photographs from UPI/Corbis-Bettmann and John Fitzgerald Kennedy Library

BOOK DESIGN BY DIANE STEVENSON OF SNAP-HAUS GRAPHICS

ISBN: 0-8362-1519-2
Library of Congress Catalog Card Number: 96-83370

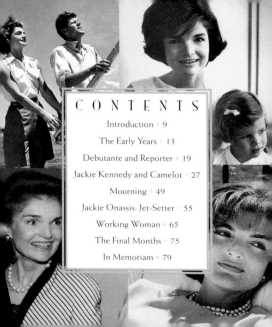

CONTENTS

JACKIE

INTRODUCTION

*I*t seems unfair and even impossible that Jacqueline Kennedy Onassis should be gone. For more than three decades her name was synonymous with elegance, sophistication, and ineffable feminine mystery. She inspired her country and indeed the world with her courage and dignity, graced thousands of magazine covers, and personally led two generations of women into a wider understanding of the traditional roles of marriage, motherhood, and the pursuit of a career.

We called her Jackie. We met her in 1959 as the soft-spoken and beautiful wife of the charismatic presidential candidate, John Fitzgerald Kennedy. As first lady, she became the country's cultural guide and mentor. Choked in sorrow, she presided over her slain husband's funeral one

thousand days after his
inauguration, and we
mourned with her.
Then we watched in
wonder as she slowly
resurrected herself,
joined the international
jet set by marrying one
of the world's richest men,
was widowed a second
time, and ultimately settled
into a quiet, fulfilling life as a mother, book editor,
cultural advocate, and, finally, grandmother.

No other modern woman captured the mind,
heart, and imagination of the world as she did.
Her death from cancer on May 19, 1994, left us
with an overwhelming sadness and an aching
void. Jackie Kennedy Onassis was an iconoclast,
a true individual who lived in the public eye but
maintained a rich private identity, who con-

tributed greatly to our world and yet remained eternally self-effacing and humble. When she passed on, the world lost a valuable leader, an important role model, and a truly remarkable woman.

THE
EARLY YEARS

When Jacqueline Lee Bouvier was born on July 28, 1929, she was six weeks late. Knowing her as we now do, it is tempting to interpret her delayed arrival as a pointed display of self-determination, one that would set the pattern of her entire life. From her earliest moments, Jackie obviously did things her own way, in her own time, and with whomever she chose.

Born into a world of privilege that included an eleven-room Manhattan apartment, a seaside country home on Long Island, her own stable of horses, and private lessons of every sort, young Jackie could hardly be considered ordinary. Yet material wealth and family connections did not protect her from the severe emotional trauma and painful loneliness that resulted when her mother, Janet Lee, separated from her husband, a drinker, gambler, and womanizer known as "Black Jack" Bouvier. Black Jack, so named because of his swarthy good looks and perennial dark tan, speculated on the stock market with borrowed money and spent his life bouncing between luxury and debt.

The strain of his devil-may-care attitude toward money and his frequent—and public—love affairs drove Janet to divorce when Jackie was eleven. In 1940 divorce was rare, and both Jackie and her younger sister, Lee, felt stigmatized to some extent. They desperately missed their charming, charismatic father, and Jackie remained passionately devoted to him for the rest of his life, despite his bouts of alcohol abuse, depression, and self-destruction. Reports suggest that she began to turn inward during her parents' divorce and to form the personality that

she would later liken to an iceberg: only a small part was visible, and the rest was hidden away from all but a select few intimate friends.

Like many wealthy girls, Jackie attended the best schools—Miss Chapin's on East End Avenue in New York City and Miss Porter's in Farmington, Connecticut, among others—but her intellectual curiosity separated her from other children. One headmistress, Miss Ethel Stringfellow, stated that Jackie had "the most inquiring mind we've had at this school in thirty-five years"; another teacher apparently found her reading a collection of Chekhov short stories—at age six! Being precocious, she rebelled against school rules, uniforms, and boredom, and was often sent to the headmistress's office for discipline.

In 1941, her mother married Hugh Dudley Auchincloss Jr., a prosperous Washington broker and member of one of America's founding—

and richest—families. This propelled Jackie into even more elite and rarefied circumstances. The family now divided its time between Merrywood, a forty-six-acre estate surrounding a Georgian manor house on the Potomac River across from Washington, D.C., and Hammersmith Farm in Newport, Rhode Island.

Jackie was sent to finishing school at Miss Porter's School in Farmington, Connecticut. There she quickly earned the nickname "Jacqueline Borgia," both because of her aloof and regal air (she brought along her horse, Danseuse) and because of her enthusiasm for European history, language, and literature, especially French. These interests would never leave her.

DEBUTANTE AND REPORTER

*I*n Miss Porter's 1947 yearbook, Jacqueline Lee Bouvier listed her ambition in life as "not to be a housewife." Yet she frequently confessed to being terrified of ending up an old maid, employed as a housemother in a boarding school like any of the several she had attended. She need not have worried: with her alluring combination of beauty, intelligence, and shyness, Jackie was constantly surrounded by suitors.

Jackie graduated from Miss Porter's in 1947. That summer, wearing a fifty-nine-dollar, off-the-rack dress, she "came out" at the Clambake Club in Newport. Igor Cassini, author of the "Cholly Knickerbocker" newspaper column on high society, immediately voted her "Deb of

the Year." Describing her as "a regal brunette who has classic features and the daintiness of Dresden porcelain," he raved that she "has poise, is soft-spoken and intelligent, everything the leading debutante should be." Though she had been mentioned in the society pages ever since she "hosted" her second birthday party, Jackie's fame as a refined, glamorous young woman grew. Even the somewhat reserved columnist Walter Winchell gushed that, though she was "blessed with the looks of a fairy-tale princess, Jackie doesn't know the meaning of the word snob."

In September of that year, she began her

higher education at the exclusive and academically rigorous Vassar College for Women in Poughkeepsie, New York. Despite a social life that took her away from school most weekends, she consistently maintained her place on the dean's list and even traveled to Paris for a year's intensive study at the Sorbonne. Returning to the United States at the end of her junior year and hungry for the cosmopolitan inducements unavailable in Poughkeepsie, Jackie transferred to George Washington University in the nation's capital. As a senior, she won *Vogue* magazine's sixteenth annual "Prix de Paris" contest, placing first among 1280 candidates. Her winning essay was on "People I Wish I Had Known." She chose Irish playwright and novelist Oscar Wilde, French poet Charles Baudelaire, and Russian ballet dancer and choreographer Sergei Diaghilev. Even though she ultimately turned down the prize in order to please her parents and remain in the States, winning it added even more luster to her impressive intellectual profile.

After earning a degree in French literature in 1951, Jackie accepted a $42.50-a-week job at the *Washington Times-Herald* and worked her way up from "gofer" to receptionist, and finally to a staff position as the "Inquiring Photographer." Though her duties consisted of inventing a question a day and then interviewing people at random for responses and taking their pictures, Jackie soon gained a reputation for her creative approach to the assignment.

Her questions included many unpredictable and original ones: Do you think the rich enjoy life more than the poor? Do you think a wife should let her husband think he's smarter than she is? Are men braver than women in the dentist's chair? How do you feel when you get a wolf whistle? If you were going to be executed tomorrow, what

would you order for your last meal on earth? Chaucer said that what women most desire is power over men; what do you think women desire most? And, somewhat prophetically, Which first lady would you most like to have been?

Approaching her mid-twenties, Jackie naturally began to consider the long-term commitment of marriage. She even became engaged to a Washington broker, John N. W. Husted Jr., but the betrothal was short-lived. Quizzed at the time by a newspaper colleague, Jack Kassowitz, on what special characteristics she sought in a potential suitor, Jackie answered, "I like men with funny noses, ears that protrude, irregular teeth, short men, skinny men, fat men. Above all, he must have a keen mind."

Shortly afterward, her relationship with John Fitzgerald Kennedy, whom she had met once during her senior year in college, rekindled and quickly intensified.

JACKIE KENNEDY
AND CAMELOT

I leaned over the asparagus and asked her for a date," quipped JFK when he was asked to describe the first moments of his love affair with his future wife. Jackie replied that the hosts, Charles and Martha Bartlett, had not served asparagus that particular night.

This small incident reveals a great deal about Jack and Jackie's courtship: Kennedy was witty, flamboyant, and boyishly charming; Bouvier was amused and reserved—a person to be reckoned with in her own right.

"He'd call me from some oyster bar up on the Cape with a great clinking of coins, to ask me out to the movies the following Wednesday," she reported. And finally, in May of 1953,

he even proposed via a transatlantic phone call.

Their early relationship was hectic in part because Jack, a thirty-four-year-old bachelor congressman from Massachusetts renowned for his magnetic effect on women, was deeply involved in campaigning and politicking; Jackie, twelve years younger, was busy writing her column for the *Times-Herald* and rejecting various smitten admirers. The two were brought together in 1951 by friends who felt they would be a perfect match. In the beginning, however, there were hesitations on both sides.

Jackie felt overwhelmed by the Kennedy clan. They were "carbonated water," in her words, whereas most families were flat, and the competitive roughhousing and game playing intimidated her. The Kennedys, for their part, were shocked that Jack would bring a girl home to the family compound in Hyannis who dared to ask of a football game, "If I get the ball, which way do I run?" The Kennedy sisters laughed at her interest in cultural matters and fashion and advised her to find another fantasy when she shyly admitted that she had dreamed of being a ballerina. Their reason? Jackie's size 10½ feet. "Maybe you better stick to soccer," they advised.

Yet she forged a deep bond with her fiancé's father, Joe, and Robert Kennedy frequently praised her for always keeping her "own identity." This was no small task amidst the Kennedys. Jackie, in turn, described Robert as "the one I'd put my hand in the fire for." Their close attachment lasted until Robert's assassination in 1968.

Part of Jackie's ambivalence about marriage to Jack was related to their headstrong personalities. "Since Jack is such a violently independent person and I, too, am so independent, this relationship will take a lot of working out," she admitted. But she happily accepted his proposal, telling the public that "what I want more than anything else in the world is to be married to him."

Her wish came true. On September 12, 1953, her stepfather, affectionately referred to

as "Uncle Hughdie," accompanied her down the aisle of St. Mary's Roman Catholic Church in Newport, Rhode Island. At least three thousand spectators crowded round the church for a glimpse of the fairy-tale bride, resplendent in a traditional white gown (designed by African-

American Anne Lowe) and heirloom veil, and her handsome prince. A reception followed at Hammersmith Farm, where thirteen hundred guests mingled under a brilliant, early-autumn sky. Not long after, the newlyweds were off to Acapulco.

Jack and Jackie Kennedy's marriage was tinged with magic, both black and white. At times they faced almost unendurable hardships, such as the tragic stillbirth of their first daughter in 1956 and the death of their son, Patrick Bouvier, in August, 1963, just two days after his birth and only three months before his father would be killed. They lived under the enormous pressure of Jack's skyrocketing political career and daily faced a worldwide public clamoring for peeks behind the thin walls of their privacy. Jack Kennedy's health was also failing: he suffered from severe back problems and Addison's disease, an anemic condition

that steadily grew more debilitating.

Yet they also shared great moments: the birth of Caroline on November 27, 1957, and John on November 25, 1960; Jack's reelection to the Senate in 1958 and his election to the presidency two years later; and Jackie's simultaneous ascent to celebrity status as the "closest thing America has to royalty."

Jackie was the perfect political wife. She campaigned with her husband, addressing his various constituents in their own languages: French, Portuguese, Spanish, or Italian. She planned his campaign schedule and supplied the literary allusions for his speeches. She commandeered a supermarket public address sys-

tem in Kenosha, Wisconsin, to encourage shoppers to vote for Jack, endured a rigorous schedule that rarely allowed them to spend two nights together, and stated, after the presidential election, that "you have to do what your husband wants you to do. My life revolves around my husband. His life is my life. It is up to me to make his home a haven, a refuge, to arrange it so that he can see as much of me and his children as possible—but never let the arrangements ruffle him, never let him see that it is work. I want to take such good care of my husband that, whatever he is doing, he can do better because he has me. His work is so important."

Nevertheless, throughout their marriage, Jackie took frequent extended trips alone, pursued her cultural interests and separate friendships, rode to the hounds (though she was advised that Americans would consider this an elitist, even offensive, pastime), and maintained a home of her own, called Wexford, in Virginia, where she could escape with the children. Her independence and her need for solitude—to sketch and paint, read and think—was legendary. Her husband never challenged it. Instead he encouraged her autonomy, affectionately and respectfully describing his wife as "fey."

In her spare time, Jackie transformed the White House and rewrote the role of president's wife, which remained one of the most glittering legacies of Camelot. As first lady, she used her sophisticated style, her elegant taste, and, most important, her respect for history and tradition to resurrect the 132-room executive mansion, which had fallen into disrepair and neglect, into a national monument and museum. She personally sorted over twenty-five thousand items stored in the basement, created the position of White House curator, and funded virtually the entire project—despite serious criticism—by supervising the creation of a picture guidebook called *The White House: An Historical Guide*, which went on sale to visitors for one dollar on July 4, 1962. It immediately generated hundreds of thousands of dollars (which today have grown to millions), all of which was channeled into renovation and restoration of the presidential domicile.

She then brought the White House into the living rooms of the world in the television production "A Tour of the White House with Mrs. John F. Kennedy," which attracted forty-six million viewers in 106 countries. Jackie filled the executive mansion with priceless art, cajoling her wealthy friends to donate paintings and sculptures, and she invited the world's leading performing artists to entertain at White House functions. Jackie also initiated plans for a White House library and the John F. Kennedy Center for the Performing Arts.

She did all this with painstaking efficiency and still zealously guarded her family's privacy. Jackie's press policy of "minimum information given with maximum politeness" and the written pledge of secrecy about Kennedy family life that she demanded from all employees were crucial, in her eyes: they allowed her to maintain a sense of self in the mad whirlwind of White House life.

She also traveled the world with her husband and often surpassed him in popularity, especially in France, where Jack endeared himself to the crowd by introducing himself as "the man who accompanied Jackie Kennedy to Paris." And she consistently charmed world leaders, even the Soviet premier Nikita Khrushchev: When he mentioned the impressive number of teachers under the communist regime in the So-

viet Ukraine, she sighed, "Oh, Mr. Chairman, don't bore me with statistics." Khrushchev was amused. At one point Jackie asked about the dogs used in the Soviet space program; Khrushchev, on his return trip home, sent her one as a gift.

She even advised her husband on matters of national and international importance and encouraged him to sign the Nuclear Test Ban Treaty. She was an exemplary first lady, the perfect "queen" for the Camelot that she, with her grace, her style, her vitality, her youth, her sense of a fabled past, and her vision of a gilded future helped to create during her husband's one thousand days as president of the United States.

Her greatest accomplishment of all, however, may have been raising Caroline and John so beautifully in the midst of such tremendous pressure: She protected them from prying pho-

tographers and reporters and created an aura of normalcy and predictability. "It isn't fair to children in the limelight to leave them to the care of others and expect they will turn out all right," she stated. "People have too many theories about rearing children. I believe simply in love, security, and discipline." She carefully

nurtured her children, identifying the most important parental act as "not to shut off the inquiring mind by being impatient with its questions. The seemingly endless chain of 'whys' means something important to the child—his way of learning."

Caroline was only six and John three when their father was murdered, so Jackie raised them to adulthood on her own. "If you bungle raising your children," she said, "I don't think whatever else you do well matters very much." She did it, as she did everything, with surpassing excellence.

MOURNING

The assassination of President John Fitzgerald Kennedy on November 22, 1963, rocked the world. In the midst of this unspeakably horrible event and its agonizing aftermath, Jackie Kennedy stood alone, the embodiment of strength, courage, and nobility of character. Suddenly Camelot ended. It was violently torn away from her, leaving the young mother to face her grief in the media's brilliant glare as the nation watched in horror and looked to her for guidance.

Her contribution during this bleak period cannot be overstated. In a Dallas hospital directly after the shooting, she refused a sedative, stating simply, "I want to be with my husband when he dies." When a kindly doctor attempted to persuade her to leave the president's body as his coffin was delivered, she calmly asked, "Do you think seeing the coffin can upset me, Doctor? I've seen my husband die, shot in my arms. His blood is all over me. How can I see anything worse than I've seen?"

And who will ever forget the image of Jackie in her bright pink suit, covered with blood standing to Lyndon Johnson's left as he took the oath of office. She had been advised to change her clothes: "Absolutely not," she said. "I want the world to see what Dallas has done to my husband." It was Jackie's fearless acceptance of the raw and ugly truth, her refusal to diminish it or to lie, that gave the American people the courage to bury their young president and go on.

Jackie Kennedy was personally responsible for every memorable—and ultimately healing—aspect of her husband's funeral. Instructing her staff to research the funerals of Andrew Jackson, Franklin Delano Roosevelt, and Abraham Lin-

coln, Jackie attended to each detail of the
solemn event. She arranged for the president's
body to lie in state in the Capitol rotunda, for
the coffin to be drawn by the same caisson used
in Roosevelt's funeral procession, for the rider-
less black horse (ironically named "Black Jack")
and young John-John's sad salute as his father's

coffin was carried past him. Jackie insisted that the honor guards stare at her husband's coffin rather than away, as is customary, and selected and placed the flowers. She chose the haunting Irish bagpipe music, requested the eternal flame, personally greeted 220 representatives from 102 nations, and even wrote a heartfelt letter of sympathy and condolence to the widow of Officer J. D. Tippit, the Dallas patrolman slain by Kennedy's alleged assassin, Lee Harvey Oswald. Asking her staff to "please be strong" and promising that "in two or three days we'll all collapse," she covered her face with a black veil, and, clutching the hands of her two young children, became a living symbol of grace under pressure.

Yet after she left the White House and moved into a Georgetown residence that instantly became a major tourist attraction and afforded her no privacy whatsoever, she confided to friends that "I'm a living wound. My life is over. I'm dried up—I have nothing more to give, and some days I can't even get out of bed. I cry all day and all night until I'm so exhausted I can't function. Then I drink."

Tormented by her memories, guilt-ridden because she felt she somehow should have saved her husband, and relentlessly pestered by her fans, Jackie finally fled to New York City, where she purchased a fifteen-room apartment on Fifth Avenue overlooking Central Park. She was desperate to establish a sense of normalcy for herself and her two children.

Jackie Kennedy was thirty-five years old.

JACKIE ONASSIS:
JET-SETTER

One year after the assassination, Jackie, still in deep mourning for her lost husband, wrote: "I think that I should have known that he was magic all along. I did know it—but I should have guessed it could not last. I should have known that it was asking too much to dream that I might have grown old with him and see our children grow up together. So now he is a legend when he would have preferred to be a man."

Obviously melancholy and not yet recovered from an incapacitating depression, Jackie declined several government positions—ambassadorships, chief of protocol, and others—offered to her by Lyndon Johnson. She preferred to live quietly with Caroline and John, to walk them to school and take them to the park for ice-cream cones. The move to New York City allowed her more privacy, which she desperately craved, and more family support. Slowly, she regained her strength, appearing in public at fund-raisers and cultural events, often with escorts who were considered "safe"—that is, above the possibility of rumor.

After living in New York for two years, her name became romantically linked to various men—Roswell Gilpatric, poet Robert Lowell, and British diplomat Lord Harlech, among others—but the public never knew the details of her reported attachments. She traveled, as always, making at least one trip—to Cambodia and Thailand in 1967—at the specific request of Robert McNamara, who hoped that Jackie's presence would help deflate anti-American sentiments born of the Vietnam War.

Jackie suffered yet another tragic blow [when] Robert F. Kennedy, her beloved brother-in[-law,] was assassinated on June 6, 1968. Enraged[, bitt]er, and helpless, she cried, "I hate this cou[ntry. I] despise America. I don't want my child[ren to] live here anymore. If they're killing Kenn[edys,] my kids are number one targets. I want t[o get] [o]ut of this country." Four months later, on [O]

ber 20, 1968, she married Greek shipping ty-
coon Aristotle Onassis.

All around the world, people expressed
cynical shock and uttered harsh judgments
against the newlyweds. They scoffed that
Onassis, twenty-nine years her senior and with
a sixth-grade education, married Jackie because
she had class and power, and that Jackie married Ari because he had millions—and millions.
Rumors spread of a complicated prenuptial
agreement that outlined Jackie's conjugal obliga-
tions as well as her considerable material gain.

In fact, at the time of her marriage, Jackie
received three million dollars, plus one million
in trust for each of her children. Her critics
forget that Onassis was her longtime friend:
Jackie had cruised aboard his 325-foot luxury
liner, the *Christina*, while recovering from the
death of her son, Patrick Bouvier. And Aristotle
Onassis had arrived at the White House to

console her within hours of Jack Kennedy's death, though this was not reported in the press at the time.

Onassis showered Jackie with gifts—more than five million dollars in jewelry alone, including an engagement ring worth over a million dollars, and he allowed her complete personal freedom. At first, Jackie was somewhat demure. "You know, everyone talks about how rich I am. I'm not really that rich. I have a few thousand in my checking account, some savings, a few stocks and bonds." Then came the clincher: "Of course there are a lot of things I can charge to Olympic Airways."

Later, her spending would surpass the limits of most people's imaginations—including Ari's. Jackie soon became a jet-set fixture: skiing in Gstaad, sunbathing nude on Onassis's private Greek island, Skorpios, flying to Paris from New York just to dine at Maxim's, obsessively shopping—sometimes buying as many as two hundred pairs of shoes for herself or 365 silk ties for Ari at a time. She had an allowance of thirty thousand dollars a month, which rarely covered her burgeoning expenses. After two years of marriage, rumors of marital discord began to emerge.

Then tragedy struck again. Ari's beloved son, Alexander, was killed in an airplane crash, and shortly afterward, his daughter, Christina, attempted suicide. Ari, unable to bear the loss and pain, abandoned the will to live. He and Jackie spent the majority of their time apart, she in New York or traveling, he in Greece or Paris, often in the company of his longtime mistress, opera legend Maria Callas.

Onassis met with lawyers to plan a divorce settlement after seven years of marriage. Before any of the legal work was finalized, however, he fell seriously ill. Jackie took him to a Paris hos-

pital. When he showed signs of strengthening, she left for a ski vacation in New Hampshire.

When Aristotle Onassis died on March 15, 1975, Jackie was in New York City. She flew immediately to Paris and then to Greece for the funeral, but Onassis's family—his daughter, Christina, and his sisters—shunned her. Nevertheless, Jackie spoke warmly of her second husband: "Aristotle Onassis rescued me at a time when my life was engulfed in shadows. He meant a lot to me. He brought me into a world where one could find both happiness and love. We lived through many beautiful experiences together which cannot be forgotten, and for which I will be eternally grateful."

After a vicious eighteen-month legal battle against Christina Onassis (who called Jackie the "Black Widow"), Jackie collected twenty-six million from the estate of her late husband.

She would not marry again.

WORKING
WOMAN

I have always lived through men. Now I realize I can't do that anymore," said Jackie after Onassis's death. Financially independent and forty-five years old, Jackie now entered perhaps the quietest phase of her life. But, as in all of the others, she would surprise the world with her unpredictable choices.

She declined an offer from Ed Koch, mayor of New York, to become the city's commissioner of cultural affairs at sixty-two thousand dollars per year, but accepted a two-hundred-dollar-a-week editorial position at Viking Press. Ignoring the scores of reporters and photographers who hounded her, Jackie reported to work four days a week, but resigned two years later when Viking published a fictional account of an assassination attempt on Ted Kennedy.

She immediately found a new home at Doubleday & Company, where she rose over time to senior editor, ultimately earning fifty thousand dollars and editing ten to twelve books a year. Jackie liked to focus on work that, as she put it, "takes me on a journey into something I didn't know before." This included a tell-all autobiography by ballerina Gelsey Kirkland called *Dancing on My Grave* (1986), Michael Jackson's 1988 autobiography, *Moonwalk*, and Bill Moyers and Joseph Campbell's *The Power of Myth*. She was also known for her meticulous attention to detail.

Commenting in 1979 on her return to work—the only one of America's fifty wealthiest women who reported to work at all—Jackie revealed to *Ms.* magazine: "What has been said for many women of my generation is that they weren't supposed to work if they had families. There they were, with the highest education, and what were they to do when the children were grown—watch the raindrops coming down the windowpane? Leave their fine minds unexercised? Of course women should work if they want to. You have to be doing something you enjoy. That is a definition of happiness: 'complete use of one's faculties along lines leading to excellence in a life affording them scope.' It applies to women as well as to men. We can't all reach it, but we can try to reach it to some degree."

Aside from her professional work, Jackie became a high-profile advocate dedicated to preserving New York City's architectural heritage. "I am passionate about architecture," she said. "We are the only country in the world that trashes its old buildings. Too late we realize how very much we need them."

In 1977 she led a protest against a proposed tower to be built over Grand Central Station. "You must help me," she demanded of the commuters from a platform. "This building is part of our heritage. It must not be deserted." She ultimately prevailed in a United States Supreme Court ruling in 1978.

Ten years later she fought a high-rise development project that would have destroyed the southwest corner and cast a long shadow over Central Park. "We are drawing the line at Columbus Circle," she stated in a news conference in the Municipal Art Society office. "It's our responsibility to voice concern when we feel the city's future is in danger."

She also saved St. Bartholomew's Episcopal Church from demolition. "The future of New York is bleak if landmark laws no longer apply to religious institutions," she announced before the Senate-Assembly Committee of New York

State. "I think that if you cut people off from what nourishes them spiritually or historically then something inside of them dies."

Just as Jackie Kennedy returned the White House to its former and intended glory, so Jacqueline Kennedy Onassis used her power and influence to save the face of her own city. The people of New York owe her a profound debt of gratitude.

On the more personal level, Jackie dated several men, including film and theater director Mike Nichols and columnist Pete Hamill. No relationship lasted, probably because, as she herself put it, "I am happiest when I'm alone." As she grew older, she seemed to turn pensive and somewhat philosophical: "I have been through a lot and I have suffered a great deal. But I have had lots of happy moments, as well. Every moment one lives is different from the other. The good, the bad, hardship, the joy, the tragedy, love, and happiness are all interwoven into one single, indescribable whole that is called life. You cannot separate the good from the bad. And perhaps there is no need to do so, either."

A decade ago, she became seriously involved with Belgian-born power broker, financier, and diamond merchant Maurice Tempelsman, a man who shuns the spotlight (though he often sits on

presidential advisory councils). Jackie and Tempelsman shared her Fifth Avenue apartment as well as her 350-acre beachfront retreat on Martha's Vineyard. They frequently sailed on his yacht, the *Relemar*, hosting such guests as Bill, Hillary, and Chelsea Clinton; and every summer, Jackie invited the entire Kennedy clan for a day of picnicking and play.

Jackie's children have grown up. Caroline, a lawyer and legal scholar, is married to Edwin Schlossberg, an artist and businessman. They have three children: Rose, Tatiana, and John. Jackie exulted in her role as grandmother, exclaiming that Caroline's children "make my spirits soar!"

John F. Kennedy Jr., also a lawyer, is a former member of the district attorney's office of New York City. Like his mother, he attempts to keep his life sedulously private. Alas, this can be difficult for a man dubbed "Prince Charming," who in 1988 was selected as *People* magazine's "Sexiest Man Alive." In September of 1995 he launched *George*, a magazine named after George Washington that focuses on the inner workings and little-known faces of politics: campaign directors, speech writers, as well as up-and-comers who may be famous soon.

THE
FINAL MONTHS

At age sixty-four, Jacqueline Bouvier Kennedy Onassis was stricken with non-Hodgkin's lymphoma, an aggressive form of cancer that spread, despite chemotherapy and steroid treatment, to her brain and liver.

Facing her own death, she revealed the same bravery and courage she had evinced years before, as when she remarked: "I'm almost glad it happened because it's given me a second life. I laugh and enjoy things so much more."

She expected a few more years ("even if I have only five, so what, I've had a great run"), but the cancer took her in a matter of months. When it became obvious that further treatment was useless, Jackie left the hospital. "I want to die at home with my family," she said.

Outside her apartment building, more than two hundred reporters gathered. When she passed on, the crowd swelled to thousands of distraught mourners. They sang "The Battle Hymn of the Republic" and spread flowers. Yet we must remember that she died, as her son told us, "surrounded by her friends and her books and the people and things she loved. And she did it in her own way, and we can all feel lucky for that, and now she's in God's hands."

Jackie Kennedy Onassis's funeral at St. Ignatius Loyola Church lasted eighty minutes, but her memory—and her legacy—is eternal. Sixty-four bells—one for each year of her life—rang out from the Washington National Cathedral as she was buried in Arlington National Cemetery beside her husband and children.

In

Memoriam

*G*od gave her very great gifts and imposed upon her great burdens. She bore them all with dignity and grace and uncommon common sense.

—President Bill Clinton

*I*n times of hope, she captured our hearts. In tragedy, her courage helped salve a nation's grief. She was an image of beauty and romance and leaves an empty place in the world as I have known it. . . . I feel a poignant sense of loss, and a larger one for the nation.

—Lady Bird Johnson

*T*he nation owes a great debt to Jacqueline Kennedy Onassis. And the nation has lost a treasure.

—HILLARY RODHAM CLINTON

*S*he showed us how one could approach tragedy with courage.

—PRESIDENT JIMMY CARTER

*S*he made a rare and noble contribution to the American spirit. But for us, most of all she was a magnificent wife, mother, grand-mother, sister, aunt, and friend. She graced our history. And for those of us who knew and loved her—she graced our lives.

—SENATOR EDWARD M. KENNEDY